Every Cent Counts

Mommy's Guide to Using Daddy's Hard-Earned Cash to Build a Dream Home

By: Sharon Turner

9781635012798

I0510872

PUBLISHERS NOTES

Disclaimer – Speedy Publishing LLC

Speedy Publishing LLC

40 E Main Street, Newark, Delaware, 19711

Contact Us: 1-888-248-4521

Website: http://www.speedypublishing.co

REPRINTED Paperback Edition: 9781635012798:

Manufactured in the United States of America

DEDICATION

To Josh. You are mommy's little man

TABLE OF CONTENTS

CHAPTER 1- STRETCHING THE FAMILY BUDGET

There comes a time in every family where we have to evaluate our spending and start looking out for the future. Times are tough and if we're not careful, we'll go through our savings only to end up back at square one.

Perhaps you haven't yet been able to save and you feel as if developing a family budget is far too difficult. Well, as a mom of six, I'm here to tell you that despite your expenses and the size of your family there are still ways to effectively budget, save money and make every dollar stretch further than ever before.

If you're struggling to make ends meet at the end of every month, or you are falling into ever-growing debt, now is the time to rework your finances so that you can improve your lifestyle and protect your family's future. Regardless of your income, there are ways to cut corners and save money.

Every Cent Counts!

Keep in mind that developing a family budget doesn't mean that you can't occasionally splurge or that you need to restrict your family in any way. In fact, it's quite the opposite.

Your mindset will be to curb spending where it's not directly benefiting your family in the long run, and to stretch, invest and make better purchase decisions. In other words, it's about making your money go further - and work harder for you and your family.

Creating a budget will also help you identify "cash leaks" quickly, and in many cases, you may not even notice where a good portion of your money is going.

We all make "routine" purchases and just based on our lifestyle choices and habits alone, we can end up spending twice as much as we really have to. For example, do you visit the grocery store more than three times a week to purchase meals and supplies for your family? If so, cutting this down to one trip a week and getting everything you need at once will instantly reduce your spending.

Not only will you purchase only what you need, but you'll be able to design your shopping around current weekly specials, so that you are taking advantage of coupons and discounts. Your budget can be as flexible as you're comfortable with as well, changing as you make more money, or as your family requires. This report was written to provide you with the ability to create a systematic process where you can easily start saving more money each month, and improving your family's lifestyle while protecting your future.

Review Your Spending to Get a Sense of Where to Cut Costs

For most of us, we're living on a fixed income where we know what to expect with each paycheck each month, and if that's the case with you, you'll find it much easier to strategically develop a budget plan for your family. If you are an entrepreneur or working in a job where your income fluctuates, you can still develop a budget but you'll need to make sure it accommodates any possible decrease in income each month.

The first step in developing a budget is to take stock of your fiscal situation. Assess exactly where you are in your financial life, taking inventory of all expenses on a month-to-month basis. When you begin to list the different expenses you have, you'll gain a better idea as to how you need to better manage your money, while identifying potential ways of saving a bit of money each month.

Remember, you don't have to save hundreds a month, but instead, work within a budget that helps you pay the bills, while putting a little aside every month. It will add up quickly.

When evaluating your expenses and spending, you need to begin by writing down your bills but make sure you also analyze bank statements and credit card accounts. You want to keep an eye out on "casual spending" where you are spending money on places that aren't really necessary.

Budgeting begins with self-evaluating your own spending, and then taking a closer look at your monthly bills to determine whether there are ways of consolidating your expenses to make it more manageable for your family. When going through your expenses and identifying key areas where you can save money, be sure to include a detailed list that segments your spending into categories.

For example, your spreadsheet could include "Obligatory Spending" such as your mortgage or rent payment, as well as "Necessities" which include food and utilities. Then, include "Pocket Expenses" including entertainment and of course, "Family Allowances" that may include family trips, clothing, home improvements, and misc. events and items. The more you create a detailed overview of your spending and overall costs, the easier it will be to identify areas where you can cut spending and save more money.

Writing your expenditures down often sheds a lot of light on areas in your financial life that could be 'tweaked', and that extra bit of money each month will go a long way.

A budget helps your entire family focus on common goals. It is unifying families in mutual purpose and effort, working together towards a successful outcome and reward. In addition, setting a family budget helps you prepare for emergencies as well as unexpected expenses.

Tip: One of the easiest ways to get the kids involved is by offering them a weekly allowance in exchange for doing odd jobs around the house, or set up a bank account for each of your children and deposits their earnings on a regular basis, showing them statements of their account growing over time. Not only will this help them learn how to budget, but also teach them a very valuable lesson about responsibility.

CHAPTER 2- CRAFTING WAYS TO BECOME FINANCIALLY STABLE

You have been through a quite tough couple of years, not to mention decade, most especially when it comes to financial. Most people from the different parts of the globe, regardless of what status they may have, are now looking for the most effective ways in order to be financially stable. There are actually quite a lot of factors for you to consider, but just so you know, achieving what you have set out to do is all about passion, dedication, and real efforts.

With the New Year upon everyone, people are all at the very beginning of their most intended New Year's resolutions. People are all trying to join the gym, eat healthier, give up alcohol, so on and so forth. Perhaps, now is also the perfect time to begin thinking about your financial overhaul, right? Well, by finance, it means products such as personal loans, credit cards, or maybe an overdraft, or any forms of finances that potentially mean that you are in debt.

Every Cent Counts!

For your New Year's financial resolution to work, there are three essential qualities that you should take into careful consideration. These are the basics that you need to take into account.

First, it should be simple. It your resolution is too complicated, chance is it won't actually happen. Thus, if you really want to maintain that resolution all year out or maybe for the next years to come, you should make it simple to make it attainable.

Second, you should also be specific about your financial resolution. Remember, vague resolutions are literally useless. It is essential that you choose or set specific resolution. For instance, it you intend to lessen your debt, you need to set a quantifiable realistic amount as well as an effective time frame. If you push your limit or try too much, chance is it won't happen. It is better to list 1 thing right than to have a long list of 10 things that you can't do or won't do.

Third, automated financial resolution is the key. You are living in a hectic and busy world. So the most effective way to ensure that all things get well done is for you to make them your priority. And the best way for you to make them your long term priority would be to essentially automate it.

These three basic factors can be the key to maintaining your pledge to fix your finances. It is that time again when you use a New Year as your excuse to revamp the different facets of your live and make your own financial resolution. For many people, New Year's resolution basically involves common aspects like fitness and health, but there are also other people who try to have some changes in order to improve their own financial health and status. Well, you should be one of them too. You know how rewarding it is to be financially stable.

Set the Target on Only One Goal

Every person wants to set goals and dream big, but actually reaching those dreams and goals can be often difficult to achieve. One crucial issue may be that you are not being specific about what you really want to reach or achieve.

It is definitely hard to start or maintain one goal if your real objectives are vague. However, by being detailed and specific about your goals, you have a better chance for success. Of course, this may come to you as a challenge to set specific goals, but getting it off on exactly the right hand with specific and real plan in hand will put you ahead, encouraging you to maintain and stick with these goals.

Financial goal setting can prove to be a challenging task for many. It is, however, essential nowadays to set a specific financial goal. Without an accurate or specific financial goal, it will become impossible for you to manage your finances and your earnings through different phases of your life. It should definitely be done considering in min the different individual requirements.

It is also essential to create your specific plan, keeping into account what you really want to reach of achieve financially. Well, this can be your first step to creating wealth. Aside from that, you should also envision yourself twenty years after. This may include your lifestyle, your kid's education, savings, and your retirement age. These are considered as the most basic goals that are present in almost all people. Planning your retirement is a very critical stage indeed.

Wealth creation and retirement planning are the two most fundamental parts of an individual's life. There are actually lots of resources that you can benefit from, resources and tools that can cater to your unique needs when it comes to setting and achieving your specific financial goal.

Another important step is to establish your short term goal. What is it that you want to be or do two to five years from now. This may include buying a car, a home, long vacation trip, or paying off your loans, and many more.

In addition to that, being specific in setting your goal is to determine what you can do on a regular or monthly basis. This is considered accomplished if you're able to effectively save enough money from your earnings or your salary. But you should not be too overwhelmed by bigger pictures.

Having a specific goal instead of a general one will definitely prove to be very beneficial and rewarding. This applies to both short term and long term goals. By being specific, you are setting the right path to achieve that specific financial goal. Be smart in creating your goals to help you be prepared and confident enough to be able to achieve whatever it is that you want to achieve. Once you truly know what you intend to have in life in financial terms, then you are on your way to becoming financially stable.

Prioritize Spending

Getting out of debts when you actually have large amount of outstanding balance creeping up can be overwhelming. Such large debts, wondering how you're going to get rid of it can lead to great stress. Trying to pay your debts and never accrue additional amount can be more stressful and inconvenient for most people. This is why it is basically essential to make paying off debts your main priority.

Sharon Turner

Realizing the real importance of paying for all your debts first should always be your priority. This realization will definitely lead you and offer you the opportunity to make your dreams of being financially stable and debt free becomes a reality. Your main goal should be to have your finances under full control, not the other way around. Once you've taken the right step of making your finances your priority, you'll become more aware about how much you're spending every month and how much you're able to save.

Everyone wants to live a debt free life, but the question is how? In the current economy situation nowadays, it's extremely difficult to live a life full of debts and at the same time manage a family's expense. So, you need to take action immediately in order to pay off your debts. The most effective way for you to live a life free of debts is to create a good budget plan. Follow this plan accordingly and clear your balances. If you want to know how to devise a plan, here's how:

Know all your debts: This is the first important take to take towards creating the plan. You should definitely identify your current debt situation in order for you to be debts free soon enough. Carefully, go through your loans, credit card statement, and other debt statements that you may have. Calculate these amounts that you owe on different loans, cards, etc. and know the exact full amount you need to repay. Though you may be surprised with the total, however, the idea is for you to discover how much you owe exactly so that you'll be able to make some arrangements accordingly.

Prioritize: Once you've totaled the amount you need to pay off, you have to prioritize payments. Consider which debts you will need to pay off immediately, and which debts can be paid later. The best step to make if you actually have lots of debts is to select those with higher interest rates. With this, paying off smaller debts will be easier for you. Some people, however, think the exact opposite.

Every Cent Counts!
They tend to prioritize smaller debts and leave the bigger ones behind.

Devise a plan: After establishing the priority list, it's time for you to devise an effective plan. A payment plan will be able to help you pay off those priority loans much easily. So, try putting all extra money for loan payments. If possible, you can even make double payment in order to lessen the amount of repayment. In terms of the smaller debts, you can always make minimum payment until you're able to pay them all.

Automatic repayment: For you to keep a debt free life, you can always consider automatic repayment system. One of the best ways to make a timely repayment of debts is to create automatic repayment of debts from your own bank account. This can actually save you lots of time, and can also assure you that all payments are paid on time.

Chapter 3- Never Let an Emergency Catch You by Surprise

If you are hit with a serious money crisis and you find yourself scrambling around for emergency money, here's how to assess your situation and get back on your feet.

All of a sudden and without warning, your roof begins to leak! Your hot water heater shuts down and your computer goes up in smoke, the clutch needs to be replaced in your car and your son decides to have his wedding on the Isle of Oahu – all of this within the same week!

As you sit, stunned and you ponder an exit strategy you receive a friendly letter from the IRS explaining that you miscalculated your taxes in 1996, and they now own your house.

The above scenario looks like a money emergency of biblical proportions. You are afraid to open your front door for fear of finding a swarm of locusts! Thank goodness, there are things you can still do to restore your financial life and equilibrium—and perhaps even fend off future misfortune—without having to sell your very soul.

Wherever there are money woes, you can be sure to find crippling emotional setback. Avoid it all you try, you might just as well begin to prepare for the devastating fiscal and the emotional fallout that is sure to come. You will need to cope very well with both if you hope to make a solid financial comeback.

Whenever a money emergency hits, it will be your ability to deal with the individual pitfalls that will hold you in good stead. It is when a series of financial hits come your way that the stress will tend to accumulate and make your life much more difficult to cope. You will not be so overwhelmed when you can calmly and rationally look at each individual problem as it arises. If you sit back wringing your hands with worry and allow all of your emergencies to pile into one; you will find yourself down for the count.

Calm must take center stage. You must NEVER allow yourself the luxury of panic. There is no one there for you to just take over. You are all you have. The more you panic, the less effective you will be. You need to keep a very clear head to be able to sit down and come up with an appropriate plan. Be aware of your own tendency to sabotage your plans further. It is only when you are at your most calm that you will be prepared to get to where you need to be and then overcome.

At even the first hint of a money emergency, it's important not to act right away. If you do you will inevitably make a mistake! First, before you can manage your finances again, you have to first manage your emotions. You absolutely must regain your balance before you can even begin to make a plan.

If your money emergency demands that you act quickly, think first about seeking the advice of a debt counselor, money coach or financial planner. Whenever possible think about seeking out the aid of a financially perceptive friend or family member who can help you to come to a clearer perspective.

Remember the old adage that "two heads are always better than just one!" You won't need to make major cash investment if you're strapped. Look for a planner who will give you a one-hour consultation for $150. Often times this will be all you will need to securely turn the corner.

The first step toward establishing financial stability is to step back, take a deep breath and assess the damage. Possibly one of the bigger mistakes people make when they're in a financial crisis is not being prepared to make a clear assessment of where they're at. You can easily become overwhelmed. However, totaling up the damage serves two important purposes. First, you need to know exactly how much you owe how much money you have in hand and what it will take to cover the distance between the two. Second, you will want to avoid any other mishaps, such as penalties, further repairs, missed deadlines, etc. If you are not properly prepared, you must become prepared on the spot.

Any type of money crisis will catch you unaware and you will feel cornered. Wouldn't it be ideal to be ready and waiting for the crisis? How likely is this to happen to you, though? Most people will be at least somewhat prepared. If the crisis is not too dire, they will be able to handle it ok. Some will be sunk from the get go. The idea is to not be overwhelmed and to have a good plan of action, no matter how little or how a lot. You need to be entirely prepared to deal with any sized setback. Ideally, those unexpected expenses could be covered by the funds in the Irregular Expenses account in any good budget.

Every Cent Counts!

Unfortunately, though, there is always a common problem. You might well have an emergency stash—but its most often depleted. This same problem affects the majority of us so take heart. At about this time many people make the mistake of turning to plastic for relief. Resist this one. You will only be transferring your problems from one pocket to the other. On the other hand, if you are sure you can handle using credit cards to deal with a cash emergency, you had better be sure you could pay them off when the time comes. Otherwise, why add yet another debt and another problem. Eventually, it will all catch up with you. If you're truly running while on your last leg, consider taking out a home equity line of credit. This will work for some. The interest is tax deductible, but those aren't fixed rates. Be smart about this remedy, though. Unless you plan to pay back the amount you borrowed promptly, it can end up costing you more than you thought—especially if you've already depleted your own equity.

Think well before borrowing from your 401(k) or IRA. There are loopholes that allow you to do so, but there are also hidden costs— never mind potential taxes, penalties and other consequences. Keep in mind that if you were to lose your job, you'd have to repay the loan immediately, or be taxed as though it was a withdrawal. This remedy could be very costly in the long run.

CHAPTER 4- HOW TO INCREASE YOUR INCOME WITHOUT RESORTING TO DEBT

• Take on a hobby that you can translate into dollars. Can you walk a neighborhood dog? Teach basket weaving? Host a dining room? Baby-sit for your sister's kids? Do Computer graphics? Consider which of your talents might be worth a few extra bucks and then go out there and do it.

• Take on a part-time job. The holidays are soon coming up, and many people supplement their salaries with part-time retail jobs. Just don't spend it all on holiday gifts and be sure to bank it into your savings.

• Spend more wisely. We all have our own ways of wasting money. Now see how you can eliminate the ones that you wouldn't miss. Just saving the dollar you would normally spend on that cup of coffee each day adds up.

• Borrow from a trusted friend or relative. The interest rate is low to nil, the cash is quick—but guilt is even higher. Be sure you have a

Every Cent Counts!

plan for how you're going to pay back the loan even before you approach them.

You can spend your precious time crying in your milk wondering why you have been singled out in this way or you can get busy and look at how this could have happened to you in the first place. You will need to face some touch answers if you want to avoid future financial crises.

Suffering a serious financial crisis is an excellent time to self-assess. Ask yourself where you went wrong, where you're not paying attention—and how you might be setting yourself up for future financial setbacks. Understanding the answers to these important questions will help you out next time around should the same befall you.

Be prepared before the crisis starts. You won't be able to anticipate every time a financial burden lands in your lap, but, if you want to be cushioned against it, you have to anticipate the unanticipated.

Be very careful. An emergency fund is set up for . . . emergencies. It's not supposed to be depleted on a whim and every month. Take a closer look at your expenses these last few months, and if you have had to lean heavily on your emergency account to pad your budget, it's time to rethink your money management issues and in a hurry.

Pay special attention. Take a page out of this lady's book...she noticed that her towels were slightly singed when she took them out of the dryer one day. Instead of calling the repair guy, she shrugged it off—until the next load caused her entire house to go up in flames. We all have these same moments where we glimpse a potential crisis hovering on the horizon and do nothing until it is all too late. Pay attention to the smaller details and avoid the larger calamities.

Plan further ahead. Your clutch is likely going to give out every 80,000 miles or so. The roof can give out every 15 to 20 years. A vacuum cleaner might give up the dust in as much as five. Avoid the obvious and pay excessively later. It is your call.

Your five-year-old desktop is getting creaky. You could wait until it dies. However, according to Murphy's Law of Money, it will expire at the worst possible moment. Either way, paying for a new computer might not be part of the budget so planning ahead gives you some control over when you take the hit. Start to plan today for what you know will be coming—come hell or high water.

CHAPTER 5- IT'S TIME TO START BUILDING YOUR EMERGENCY FUND

Finding money during an emergency can be very difficult if you fail to plan. Establish emergency savings in both good times and in bad. The chance is very good that you will be called upon to put out a sum of money on the spot and when you least expect it.

It is a very good rule of thumb to sock away three to six months' living expenses. You can also use this same money when you're faced with major, unplanned expenses such as a car that breaks down or much needed college funds. The purpose of this type of savings plan is to put the money away consistently, and then tap into it for true emergencies. The success of this type of long-range savings plan will depend less on the rate of return than on, day-by-day, putting the money away and then leaving it there for a true emergency. Lock it away and then hide the key.

People who are living on a fixed-income will have the toughest time setting aside money for emergencies. If you can manage to just squeeze out another $10 or $20 each month and sock it away into a money market account, it's worth doing.

If you decide you need $2,000 in an emergency fund, look at what you can afford to sacrifice each month from your current budget and then look at that sum of money as a bill to pay yourself. Decide on a monthly amount and then put that same amount aside every month and then watch it grow. Once you have reached your goal of $2,000 you'll now be in the habit of putting away that extra set amount each month. Keep on doing it.

Financial planners echo the idea of treating your emergency fund as a bill. Put the money away each month, but don't be tempted by the latest sale. You are not to touch the amount, except for in an emergency. Putting money aside on your own is hard. Retirement plans are successful because the money comes out of your paycheck before you can get your hands on it and because there are taxes and penalties for early withdrawals.

Stashing money away in an easy access money market account takes discipline. Limit your access to the emergency fund. You can have immediate access to some of the money, but not all of it. The bulk of the fund is to be used, strictly, for emergencies and nothing else. .

Once you have saved up about two months of living expenses, move one month of expenses to a one-month CD. When the CD matures, roll the principal and interest into another one-month CD. Your savings will grow well this way. As you continue making regular payments to the emergency fund money market account, you will soon have another month of living expenses that can be used to invest in a two-or three-month CD. If you are wishing to set aside six months of expenses, continue the process until you can comfortably purchase a six-month CD. Your savings will accumulate quickly this way.

Here are the steps to begin building your emergency stash:

How much money are you willing to set aside each month?

Before you start stashing away your money for an emergency, the first step in building your emergency fund is to figure out just how much money you have to put aside in the first place.

Bye Plastic Cards!

Credit cards are perhaps one of the most expensive forms of money. A very good rule of thumb is, unless you pay off your credit card bills each month, don't use the cards for anything you can either eat or wear.

Another good rule of thumb is to consolidate your debt. If you have several credit cards, each at different rates of interest, why not fold them into a home equity loan and then write off the interest payments? This is a good way to begin an emergency savings fund.

Trim your budget

Here are some good suggestions for budget trimming that can work for just about everyone:

When mortgage rates are especially low-consider refinancing your mortgage and, while you're at it, your car loans, too.

When you live in an area that has good public transportation, see if you can get by on one car instead of two.

Make your current car last. With good maintenance, you will be able to replace it every six to eight years instead of every three years.

Do a periodic energy check on the house. Replace all essentials such as cracked storm windows and renew the weather stripping.

Cancel subscriptions to magazines or newspapers that you're not reading.

Eat out less often and learn to be creative using leftovers. If you stop for a morning cup of coffee at the local Deli, make coffee at home.

For the kids weekly allowance cut it back. Explain to them that every member of the family needs to contribute to the emergency fund for it to work.

Saving money on your own brings many rewards, and like most other things, it becomes easier over time. In the end, your entire family will have peace of mind that comes from knowing you have financial resources set up and ready for when times are the toughest. The sacrifices you make now will be realized when you need the most comfort as a family.

Adding Funds to Your Emergency Stash

If your plan for money for your next emergency is to scoop up the change that falls between the cushions, you might want to come up with a plan to add to that stash. It is always a good idea to have a little extra green for the lean times. Rainy days could be just around the corner. Rainy day funds become necessary! Here are some very clever and virtually painless ways to put aside some money now!

Every Cent Counts!

Put aside a large envelope, cookie tin, coffee jar or something similar. At the end of every week, throw a couple of dollars aside. By the end of your first month you should have some extra cash put aside to have a nice start on an emergency fund. The idea is to not count it or spend it. Place it somewhere that is hidden away. Put it somewhere that you won't be tempted to dip into it. This kind of money really adds up!

The next time you treat yourself or your family to a meal out, tip yourself! Just as you go to tip the waitress 15 to 20 percent, put the same amount aside for yourself. When you get home, stash it away in your cookie jar. Every time you go through a fast food window, put a dollar away for that cookie jar, too!

The next time you get a good raise, instead of applying it to your cost of living, bank it! This way you will always be living one raise behind and your bank account will be growing by some 3 percent.

Take advantage of that cash back option! Next time you make a purchase using your debit card, ask for a small amount of cash back. Instead of spending it, stash it away in your cookie jar! Chances are you won't even miss that extra $1, $2 or $5 bill and come emergency time, you will notice how the amount has piled up.

Next time you pay off that big-ticket item like a new car or tuition, continue to make the payments to yourself! Set up a savings account and each month slip the ghost payment into it. Watch as it builds nicely.

If you have noticed that you can get a better long distance telephone plan and you want to switch, allocate the savings to your cookie jar. You won't likely miss that little bit of extra money, and you will have a better telephone plan, too.

Consider joining a Christmas club. You will save a lot of money. Each year you put aside a bit of money and place it into a hamper program. Then, as Christmas rolls around you don't need to scramble looking for Christmas cheer to share with your family. Your hamper arrives filled to the brim with all kinds of seasonal goodies that you paid for over the previous year. You can easily put aside $50 each year towards your emergency fund this way and you and your family will enjoy a hassle free Christmas.

Sign up for a grocery shopping membership card. At the bottom of your store receipt, you will see a print out that states how much you save each week. It really adds up. You can easily save an average of $15 on each weekly grocery trip. Add that amount, each week, to your savings cookie jar.

Did you enjoy your tax refund this year? Sure you did, we all did. That's because of the new tax laws. Many people will have a little extra money coming their way after April 15. Decide to deposit that extra money right away into your savings account or cash it and then stash it. Sure you can come up with plenty of ways you can use that money now, but put it away for later. You might need it even more soon.

If you are a responsible spender, take out a credit card that rewards your loyalty. When you pay off the bill every month, use a card that promises a cash reward and bank the money. Use your reward credit card smartly and you could end up with a very nice windfall for your rainy day fund.

Put aside a large mouthed jar in the kitchen. It is very likely that your parents and grandparents had one. At the end of each workday simply empty your pockets or clean out your change purse. All the change goes into the jar. Who wants to carry around all that dead weight, anyway? Your spare change adds up a lot faster than you think. While you are at it, add at least one bill to your change jar at the end of each week. Aim for a $20!

Is it time to give up that nasty smoking habit? Imagine the money you will save! If you are not quite ready to quit at least cut back by half. Put the savings each day into your change jar and watch it overflow!

Convert to a coin-operated laundry. Keep a jar on your washer and dryer and every time you go to do a load of laundry, slip in a coin or two. This adds up month by month.

The next time you go to return a movie rental on time, pay yourself the late fee. You will see how quickly that $1.50 to $4 can add up.

If you yearn to lose some weight, try rewarding yourself the cost of the item that you do without each day. Put that money into your change jar. You will look great and you will be saving for a rainy day!

Place a large jar by the telephone. Everyone must drop in a coin to make a call. All proceeds go to the emergency fund. This one works! Emergencies always crop up. They are always guaranteed, unlike the money to deal with them. Be prepared and plan!

CHAPTER 6- AN ENERGY EFFICIENT HOME IS A FRUGAL HOME

The first step to taking a whole house energy efficiency approach is to find out which parts of your house use the most energy. A home energy audit will pinpoint those areas and suggest the most effective measures for cutting your energy costs. You can conduct a simple home energy audit yourself, you can contact your local utility, or you can call an independent energy auditor for a more comprehensive examination.

Energy Auditing Tips

• Check the insulation levels in your attic, exterior and basement walls, ceilings, floors, and crawl spaces.

Every Cent Counts!

• Check for holes or cracks around your walls, ceilings, windows, doors, light and plumbing fixtures, switches, and electrical outlets that can leak air into or out of your home.

• Check for open fireplace dampers.

• Make sure your appliances and heating and cooling systems are properly maintained. Check your owner's manuals for the recommended maintenance.

• Study your family's lighting needs and use patterns, paying special attention to high-use areas such as the living room, kitchen, and outside lighting. Look for ways to use lighting controls—like occupancy sensors, dimmers, or timers—to reduce lighting energy use, and replace standard (also called incandescent) light bulbs and fixtures with compact or standard fluorescent lamps.

Formulating Your Plan

After you have identified where your home is losing energy, assign priorities by asking yourself a few important questions:

• How much money do you spend on energy?

• Where are your greatest energy losses?

• How long will it take for an investment in energy efficiency to pay for itself in energy cost savings?

• Do the energy saving measures provide additional benefits that are important to you (for example, increased comfort from installing double-paned, efficient windows)?

• How long do you plan to own your current home?

• Can you do the job yourself or will you need to hire a contractor?

• What is your budget and how much time do you have to spend on maintenance and repair?

How Do You Use Energy at Home?

Heating accounts for the biggest chunk of a typical utility bill. Once you assign priorities to your energy needs, you can form a whole house efficiency plan. Your plan will provide you with a strategy for making smart purchases and home improvements that maximize energy efficiency and save the most money.

Another option is to get the advice of a professional. Many utilities conduct energy audits for free or for a small charge. For a fee, a professional contractor will analyze how well your home's energy systems work together and compare the analysis to your utility bills. He or she will use a variety of equipment such as blower doors, infrared cameras, and surface thermometers to find leaks and drafts.

After gathering information about your home, the contractor or auditor will give you a list of recommendations for cost effective energy improvements and enhanced comfort and safety. A good contractor will also calculate the return on your investment in high efficiency equipment compared with standard equipment.

Tips for Finding a Contractor

• Ask neighbors and friends for recommendations

• Look in the Yellow Pages

• Focus on local companies

Every Cent Counts!

• Look for licensed, insured contractors

• Get three bids with details in writing

• Ask about previous experience

• Check references

• Check with the Better Business Bureau

Checking your home's insulation is one of the fastest and most cost efficient ways to use a whole house approach to reduce energy waste and make the most of your energy dollars. A good insulating system includes a combination of products and construction techniques that protect a home from outside temperatures—hot and cold, protect it against air leaks, and control moisture. You can increase the comfort of your home while reducing your heating and cooling needs by up to 30% by investing just a few hundred dollars in proper insulation and sealing air leaks.

Insulation

First, check the insulation in your attic, ceilings, exterior and basement walls, floors, and crawl spaces to see if it meets the levels recommended for your area. Insulation is measured in R-values—the higher the R-value, the better your walls and roof will resist the transfer of heat. DOE recommends ranges of R-values based on local heating and cooling costs and climate conditions in different areas of the nation. State and local codes in some parts of the country may require lower R-values than the DOE recommendations.

Where to Insulate

Adding insulation in the areas shown below may be the best way to improve your home's energy efficiency.

- Crawl space
- Basement
- Attic
- Walls
- Floors

For customized insulation recommendations, check out the Zip Code Insulation Calculator, which lists the most economic insulation levels for your new or existing home based on your zip code and other basic information about your home.

Although insulation can be made from a variety of materials, it usually comes in four types; each type has different characteristics.

Rolls and batts—or blankets—are flexible products made from mineral fibers, such as fiberglass and rock wool. They are available in widths suited to standard spacing of wall studs and attic or floor joists.

2x4 walls can hold R-13 or R-15 batts; 2x6 walls can have R-19or R-21 products.

Loose-fill insulation—usually made of fiberglass, rock wool, or cellulose comes in shreds, granules, or nodules. These small particles should be blown into spaces using special pneumatic equipment. The blown-in material conforms readily to building cavities and attics. Therefore, loose-fill insulation is well suited for places where it is difficult to install other types of insulation.

Every Cent Counts!

Rigid foam insulation—foam insulation typically is more expensive than fiber insulation. But it's very effective in buildings with space limitations and where higher R-values are needed. Foam insulation R-values range from R-4 to R-6.5 per inch of thickness (2.54 cm), which is up to 2 times greater than most other insulating materials of the same thickness.

Foam-in-place insulation—can be blown into walls and reduces air leakage.

Should You Insulate?

The answer is probably "yes" if you:

• Have an older home and haven't added insulation. Only 20% of homes built before 1980 are well insulated.

• Are uncomfortably cold in the winter or hot in the summer—adding insulation creates a more uniform temperature and increases comfort.

• Build a new home, addition, or install new siding or roofing.

• Pay high energy bills.

• Are bothered by noise from outside—insulation muffles sound.

One of the most cost-effective ways to make your home more comfortable year-round is to add insulation to your attic. Adding insulation to the attic is relatively easy and very cost effective. To find out if you have enough attic insulation, measure the thickness of the insulation. If it is less than R-22 (7 inches of fiber glass or rock wool or 6 inches of cellulose), you could probably benefit by adding more. Most U.S. homes should have between R-22 and R-49 insulation in the attic.

If your attic has enough insulation and your home still feels drafty and cold in the winter or too warm in the summer, chances are you need to add insulation to the exterior walls as well. This is a more expensive measure that usually requires a contractor, but it may be worth the cost if you live in a very hot or cold climate.

You may also need to add insulation to your crawl space. Either the walls of the crawl space or the floor above the crawl space should be insulated.

Long-Term Savings for Heating and Cooling

Heating and cooling your home uses more energy and drains more energy dollars than any other system in your home. Typically, 61% of your utility bill goes for heating and cooling. What's more, heating and cooling systems in the United States together emit over a half billion tons of carbon dioxide into the atmosphere each year, adding to global warming. They also generate about 24% of the nation's sulfur dioxide and 12% of the nitrogen oxides, the chief ingredients in acid rain.

No matter what kind of heating, ventilation, and air-conditioning system you have in your house, you can save money and increase your comfort by properly maintaining and upgrading your equipment. But remember, an energy-efficient furnace alone will not have as great an impact on your energy bills as using the whole-house approach.

By combining proper equipment maintenance and upgrades with appropriate insulation, air sealing, and thermostat settings, you can cut your energy bills and your pollution output in half.

CHAPTER 7- HOW TO START SAVING

Nowadays, people have actually become more money wise and start planning on for their retirement after they got a job. That is the very reason why most people are always on the lookout for the most effective options available when it comes to retirement benefits. There are lots of contracts that are recognized by state government offering great benefits to the working people, most specifically when they leave their company.

Getting prepared to plan a life after retirement does not mean that you need to stay at home tending for the garden and read books all the time. Yes, you can actually sit and relax at home, but just so you know you can easily earn enough money too as you do just that. Retirement doesn't mean that you're incapacitated, incapable of doing work anymore; it is only that you need to formally and professionally leave your company that you've been doing business with or working for.

Invest and Start Early: If you're like most Americans, planning on your retirement must start on you very first job. You have to basically take advantage of the most essential steps of financial planning that anyone can make: invest carefully on a retirement account. Most employers will provide a percentage, and the best thing to do for you to ensure a comfortable and satisfying retirement is to invest on your retirement as early as possible.

This isn't the only effective way of saving money for your retirement, but it's most certainly is among the most lucrative and easiest steps that you can take to have your long awaited comfortable retirement.

Living and Lifestyle Arrangements: Next, you should look at your current lifestyle and consider the lifestyle you intend to have after your retirement. If you want to travel frequently, budget accordingly. Do you plan on moving closer to a family upon retirement? Consider the different factors and elements which are important for you - it is wise to choose only two to three situations that you want to achieve and indulge with after retirement. While everyone will experience major challenges, it is still good to have the perspectives.

Identify What You Really Need: For financial advices, this is among the cornerstones. Knowing the different resources that you actually need upon retiring is the fundamental key to having a successful and comfortable retirement. Set specific saving goals. Think ahead, instead of thinking short term. Remember, you can't save enough money for your retirement if you don't know exactly how much you need.

Savings Review and Annual Portfolio: At every year end, it is critical that you review your 401K, IRA, savings, and other types of investments you have created for your retirement. With the help of a reliable personal banker, accountant, or financial advisor, see if you're able to successfully invest anymore to your retirement. By doing so, you are maximizing retirement allotment.

Planning ahead and very carefully for retirement does not have to be time consuming or costly, but the possible dividends can prove to be substantial in the end. An accurate, solid plan begins with specific financial goals, short term or long term, and learning what it actually takes in order to achieve those goals. Reviewing your retirement account and your plan yearly will keep you updated on how you're doing on your goals.

Have You Tried Automatic Savings Plans?

The benefits of saving money are many. You do not have to be equipped with an Economics degree to understand about this concept. It has long been around from the time when money was printed. Saving money, especially in case of economic struggles is extremely important. However, it can actually be one of the most challenging tasks. You can never know for sure if you are going to be a victim of potential layoff, or getting cut for hours at work. Having enough savings that can help you and your family survive troubling times is indeed one of the smartest moves you can take.

If you are looking for an effective means of saving, well an automatic savings plan can be the best options. But what is it exactly? It's a type of savings system in which you automatically deposit fixed amount of money and at specific intervals to your investment account.

Most people save money just as an afterthought. When you receive your income, the money is being allocated to mortgage or rent, bills, daily expenses, groceries, among others. The only chance you will be adding money into your savings is only when there's money left. Unfortunately, often there is never any amount of money left to save.

Thanks to the modern technology, it is now easy to start up your own automatic savings plan. If you actually have a direct deposit via you employer, you will discover one easy way of establishing this is for you to have parts of your income or paycheck straightly directed to a savings account. It does not matter if you are able to save 10 dollars of 500 dollars, simple being able to save money automatically will guarantee you that part of your paycheck is being saved every time you're being paid.

Automatic savings plans have other advantages than the convenience and benefits of not having to deposit money manually to your account every month. Well, this kind of savings system makes it more convenient and easier for you to establish a strict personal budget, since it's more difficult to dip into the savings or overspend once the money is automatically deducted from your paycheck. This system also aid investors to continue saving money into their portfolios. So, what now? Is it beneficial to have your own automatic savings plan?

If you have successfully saved money, you are rest assured that you will be able to surpass most challenging times, enabling you and your family to have a better life. Many people argue that to have a nest egg isn't the only means that you have to take. They believe that they also have to invest the money to something. However, saving money proves to be a very smart and effective investment alone. Instead of using the money, you're saving them for later purposes. Investing on something may only risk your money but if you take it for savings, you have the money in any case.

Every Cent Counts!
Planning Emergency Savings

You are ready but you feel at a loss as to how you will come up with that extra money. You are already barely eking out a living. You can manage if you train yourself to think differently. That is the first part of any good plan.

You have to think right. If you don't think right towards your money, you won't be able to manage it.

Your First Step: Rethink how you think about money

Saving money is a calm state of mind. Before you can even begin, you have to say NO to all of the spending—and stop thinking that you actually need all the stuff you're spending all of your hard-earned money on. Just don't spend.

That is simple enough! Say NO to all of the excuses and reasons for why you feel you MUST spend. Tell yourself, NO MORE EXCUSES, PERIOD! The very next time you want to buy something, take the $50 or $100 out of your wallet, instead and stash it away somewhere. Do you see the logic? That's why you call saving. You don't end up with stuff; you end up with the hard-earned MONEY.

Another new way of thinking will be to think of frugality as your savior. Become a confirmed cheapskate and do as your most frugal friends do. Pay special note to the fact that frugal friends fix the shower curtain instead of buying a new one. Sit down with Depression-era relatives and ask about how they made ends meet despite even desperate times. You want to learn to economize.

The next step in rethinking is to become inspired. Spend all of your spare time online and search out those frugal Web sites. Look at "living cheaply," "frugal living" and "voluntary simplicity." You'll find a ton of good Web sites devoted to living on less, such as: thefrugalshopper.com, simpleliving.net and frugaliving.com.

Learn to turn shopping time into activity time. Go for a bike ride, walk down memory lane, take the kids to the park; do anything and everything that you can to take your mind off shopping and spending. It works!

Step # 2: Time to Save!

There are a number of creative ways to live on less. However, you don't want to make your life miserable. Here are some great ways to economize without missing quality of life.

Don't think too much about it – just do it! Direct deposit is now your best friend! Your money is whisked away into your IRA, 401(k) or money market account—and you don't have to do a thing to make it happen. Just drop by your payroll department and/or your bank and fill out the forms. Do it today. Eat meatless some of the time. Go veggie. Prepare just three meatless days a week (without substituting pricey fish) and you could save $25 a week, which equals $100 a month, which equals $1,200 a year! Beans: You will learn to love them.

Play the money game. Whenever you get a $5 bill, put it aside for later. Alternatively, do the same with ones, with quarters or even all your spare change. You'll have a nest egg built up before you even miss a nickel. Never spend the extras. Save all of your income-tax refund, your holiday money from the folks, the $20.38 overpayment check from the telephone company and any other extras and save every penny.

Negotiate and Haggle. You will be impressed by who will drop their prices, fees and interest rates: airlines, hotels, credit card companies, and even computer/appliance/rug salespeople. Before you even think about paying full price, haggle first.

Re-evaluate your money before you spend. That dinner out for the family will cost more than you spend on groceries in a week. That fancy pair of shoes is worth half the cost of a commuter pass. Learn what your money is worth to you, and you won't be so quick to dispose of it.

Don't overpay on your taxes. Yes, you love to get a big refund from the IRS every spring. The fact is, though, you're effectively lending money to the government and interest-free. Go through your tax return and see if you can hold out until Dec. 31 to maybe get a $150 refund. That way you can use your money NOW should you need it for an emergency and bank the refund when you get it later.

Decide to raise your insurance deductibles. Reassess each of the deductibles for your various kinds of insurance. If you can raise them at all, your premiums will drop.

Bring your mortgage costs down. Look at whether or not the rate is too high. If it is, look to refinancing – this will save you money. Now, let's look at the private mortgage insurance (PMI) you've been paying because you didn't have enough money to make a 20% down payment. If the equity in your home is greater than 22%, make sure that it is cancelled. It's the law. Finally, pay up on your mortgage. If you can manage an extra $100 per month, you will save thousands in interest costs over the long haul.

Toss out those nasty, glossy catalogs. The best-known form of spending temptation known to man or woman is the catalogs. Sure they are fun and look good, but are they worth the risk of spending? Chuck them straight out into the trash.

Refuse those unnecessary fees. Like the $2.50 you pay just because the ATM is right there, right now as opposed to walking two blocks to your bank, where you don't get charged at all every time you use your cash card. Alternatively, how about the late fees for returning videos? These really add up. Don't forget those fat charges banks hit you with when you write a check that, well, bounces.

Clean it yourself. I've discovered a very cool trick: When a clothing label says, "Dry Clean Only," I wash it. On the other hand, dab out that little mustard stain with an old-fashioned cleaning device cleverly known as a sponge.

Don't pay for a pro. If you can fix the neighbor's garage door and she can paint the kitchen: go for it and save.

Put your raise in the bank. Put that tiny 3% to 5% boost in the paycheck on your direct deposit and live on your previous salary.

Pay smart for long-distance. Evaluate all of the different telephone plans for value. Pay attention to what you are currently paying per minute. Some dial around codes or cheap calling cards (one without a surcharge per call) may give you a better rate. Not only will you save, but also you may find you won't need to speak to Alvin in Schenectady so often.

Just buy the basics for the pets. Say no to pet pampering. Does your dog need those T-bone snacks? Does your cat need that rabbit-fur-lined toy? Probably not.

Vow never again to pay full price. The next time you must shop, hop onto the World Wide Web. Look for eBay, half.com and craigslist.org for excellent sources of "lightly used" goods—

Every Cent Counts!
everything from books to jewelry to office furniture—even the entire first season of Star Trek on video.

When you are focused on being savings minded, you're thinking about money changes. Before you know it, you have substantial savings.

CHAPTER 8- HOW TO LIVE SATISFIED ON A FIXED MONTHLY BUDGET

Regardless of the time in history and no matter what the current state of the economy, no matter what the current trends are, no matter what the unemployment rate is or where interest rates are, some money-saving ideas always work and stay true.

Big changes come from small steps and if you determine to put even one of these many savings secrets into place, you will see big change in your life. You will now learn a variety of savings tips. You will learn how to best place your hard-earned money in a variety of down-to-earth ways. What you will learn about will set you up nicely in your day to day life.

Money Saving Tip #1:

The great Albert Einstein once said, "It takes a genius to see the obvious." Let these wise words guide you today. What he meant by that is that sometimes the simpler things in life are the most powerful ... but because they are so obvious, we tend to ignore them, and not let them work for us.

One of the most powerful money making ideas is this: keep a daily diary of everything you spend. Go to the dollar store, buy a little book, and carry it with you wherever you go. Write down every penny – each single penny - you spend. It's just as simple as that. If you do this one thing, you will find that something magical happens in your financial life in only a few weeks.

There is something incredibly powerful about writing down each of your expenditures. It makes the flow of money through your life more realistic and exacting. It shows you simply and clearly just exactly where you are spending your money, on what and why. Once you know this, it becomes much easier to control your spending. You will feel empowered with self-control and this will encourage saving.

Many people who have taken up this practice have not only learned something about themselves, which they never before understood, but they are often astounded by the simplicity of the lesson learned.

For example, a person could realize through examining their notebook that they actually spent nearly $1,000 throughout the year on diet soft drinks, snacks and candy bars! Since their job only brings in $20,000 per year, they realized that 5% of their entire income was being frittered away on something entirely frivolous. The person gave up the snacks and drinks, and found they had enough money to go on vacation the following year. If you had the choice between snacks and a much-needed vacation, which would you choose? Of course you would choose the vacation, we all would.

The point is it was their daily expense log that helped achieve the insight and clarity they needed to realize control of their finances. That's what a simple spending record will do for you - it will give you much needed control over your spending, and thus your financial life. There may be nothing but a 75-cent notebook and a ballpoint pen between your life of financial struggle and financial freedom.

Money Saving Tip #2:

Stop deficit spending! We all know how Uncle Sam has been creating debt— spending more money than our country takes in. It's called deficit spending. Well, don't do the same! The same rules apply to you and me. Using those nasty little plastic cards may be the "American Way," but it's a debt making way and creates plenty of fools each new day.

Today, the average credit card holder is carrying around $8,000 in plastic debt! Spending yourself into such debt with a credit card is certainly very easy, as many of you already know. The reason is psychological. When you give that clerk a credit card, it's just not the same as handing over a stack of green dollar bills. Would you as readily hand over a pocketful of ten-dollar bills as toss a credit card across a counter? Probably not. This one is a no-brainer for most!

Credit cards put you in debt and keep you there. Even for people with good incomes, paying your credit card debt down to zero can be amazingly difficult. In addition, make no bones about it; credit card debt will sap your financial strength just as readily as an open vein will deplete your physical body of its very life force. Using a credit card by choice can quickly turn to using it for need. Once you get to that point, you are already in trouble and it becomes time to get some help.

Every Cent Counts!

There is no secret in freeing yourself from the credit card game. You must take out a pair of scissors today, cut your cards in half, and begin paying them back, slowly but surely. Be sure to always pay more than the minimum amount due, even if it is only $10 more.

Once you stop adding to the debt, even small payments will eventually, add up. You can get out of debt, if you are patient and self-disciplined. Once your cards are history, you must adopt a strict pay-as-you go policy. Instead of buying now and paying later, save now and buy when you have the full amount. This is the key to being able to save.

Once again, stopping credit-oriented consuming is one of the most powerful financial tools available to anyone today. Why not pick up this tool and use it for yourself?

Money Saving Tip #3:

Sell all of your junk. That's right; it's high past time for a serious yard sale. Search throughout your house or apartment for every single item that you don't really need, and then sell it all! Every last piece!

Take an inventory. The truth is most people are astounded by what they own - and how much money they have tied up in items they no longer need and use. Why let it just sit and collect dust while it could collect interest instead in a savings account? You could easily be $600, $1,200 ... even $5,000 richer by the end of the week. As an added bonus, you'd have your place cleaned up, and you will have a fresh feeling of beginning all over again. A garage sale is an excellent way to start. Not only do you clean out your house, but also it often gives a psychological boost that helps people get control of their life and money.

Money Saving Tip #4:

Ben Franklin said long ago: "A penny saved is a penny earned." Yes, it's still true and still one of the most powerful moneymaking tips in all of history. Understood well within Franklin's famous statement is the difficulty of saving.

It's tough to save and much easier to spend! We all know that! That's why every penny saved truly is earned - because it takes so much effort to hold on to that cash! If you can do it, it will work magic in your life. Having a savings account will de-stress your life. Imagine being ahead of your bills, rather than behind. When you are ahead of your bills, you entire life comes under your own control. You sleep better at night. Your mind is freer to come up with new ways to make more money and save more. Saving is contagious - once you let it get started!

CHAPTER 9- HUGE SAVINGS TIPS: NOT FOR THE FAINT-HEARTED!

Tilt the wheel of creating wealth in your favor. Naturally, spending less is one way. However, to be sure to make your money work harder for you—set goals to make certain it happens. Many have wondered what can be the foolproof way of creating wealth. Is it to buy top paying Internet stocks or to work for a tech startup that offers you valuable stock options? Is the trick to count every penny or is the road to wealth paved with risk? Do you have to be especially smart and well-connected? Alternatively, is becoming wealthy a matter of luck?

The answer is: There is no one, true road to wealth, and all of the above have created wealth for more than just a few notable individuals. Nevertheless, you can put the odds of creating wealth on your side by following a few simple precepts.

Spend less than what you earn.

This can be the most overlooked scenario, because many people believe it's a matter of cutting back on your current standard of living—a strategy that's far too difficult for many people. Yes, you can affect your personal balance sheet by spending less money eating out or on entertaining out. Making a pot of coffee at the office instead of buying a $3 espresso will make a small difference in your cash flow. Nevertheless, the biggest difference will be made on the income side of the ledger.

If you wish to get on the right road to saving, stop looking at your budget as a pie that must be cut up into various size pieces. Instead, of trying to figure out how the different pieces will cover your expenses, concentrate on how you will expand the size of the pie. Yes, you could ask your boss for a raise. At the same time, figure out how you can begin to earn more money on the side. Start thinking about how you will sweeten the existing pie. Think about how you're spending your time, as well as your money. Perhaps instead of taking the family out this weekend, you could earn an extra $80 by becoming a waiter or bartender. Instead of taking the kids shopping at the mall, you could work as a salesclerk earning some extra cash.

If you don't wish to work every weekend, think about working every other weekend to start. Instead of paying for a baby sitter while you attend a concert, take care of a few other children on Saturday or Sunday, freeing working parents to do their errands. When it comes your weekend to work, do a switch. This will save you time and money. Then, instead of spending the extra money you earn from your part-time work, you can invest it so the money can work for you. When you do this, you will learn to appreciate your free time that much more.

Every Cent Counts!
1. Make your money work for you.

The ultimate secret to financial success lies in having your money do the work, so you can relax. This requires accumulating enough investment dollars so that the growth and earnings can free you from the need to work even harder. The last thing you will want to be doing is punching a time clock. Plenty of very wealthy people continue on working simply because they enjoy what they're doing so much. They also redefine work to include managing their money.

For the wealthy, the two can go hand in hand. Everywhere you go you will hear, "I never get to the point where I won't have to return to work because I can't afford to set money aside today. These people overlook the power of compound interest.

Every worker with earned income is now entitled to open a non-deductible IRA or, even better, a Roth IRA. The maximum $3,000-a-year contribution works out to a cost of $57.69 a week. Any hard working American is capable of achieving this goal. Moreover, a $3,000 annual investment in a Roth IRA, growing tax-free at the historical average of 10.6% for the stock market, builds to more than $500,000 in 30 years. If you start in your twenties and put $3,000 in that same Roth IRA every year, at 10.6%, you could have a nest egg of nearly, $5.2 million at age 70, according to the MSN Money's Savings Calculator. Even with an 8% annual return, you'll end up with $1.9 million.

2. Be sure your money is working for you, instead of against you.

Your money can work very powerfully for you if you make the right decisions and implement a plan of regular investing. At the same time, wrong money decisions will place deep potholes on your road to success. The classic example is credit-card debt. Consider the example of a person who charges $2,000 on a credit card at 19.8% interest and a $40 annual fee. If you make only the minimum monthly payments (and many people do just that), it will take you 31 years and two months to pay off the balance! Moreover, along the way, you'll pay an additional $8,202 in finance charges. This is absurd logic!

What could possibly be so important to charge today that it puts you in debt for a period far longer than the object is likely to last? (Sure, a mortgage lasts 30 years, but the interest is deductible and your home should grow in value over that time.) Most things that you want to charge on your card have a far shorter life. For many, they can do entirely without that one purchase.

If you're already in debt, if you would only double the minimum monthly payment, you could be out of debt in less than three years. Paying down current debt is the smartest way to start on the road to financial freedom.

3. Keep a tight clasp on that wallet.

When you take a close look at your paycheck, you'll notice many deductions before you get to the amount you can cash or put in the bank. Surely, there are deductions for Social Security, federal, and perhaps state income taxes. It's money that's out of your paycheck before you have a chance to even make decisions about it. Money set aside for wealth building should be treated in the exact same way. If your company offers a 401(k) retirement plan, make sure you sign up for the maximum possible contribution. It will be taken out of your paycheck, each pay period, automatically. (And if your company matches all or part of your contribution, failing to sign up is like walking away from free money!)

Every Cent Counts!

If you didn't have a chance for automatic deductions to a company savings plan or even a U.S. Savings Bonds payroll deduction plan, then you'll have to create your own automatic savings plan. Ask if your company will deposit your paycheck directly into your bank account—or promise yourself to do it the day you receive the check. Then sign up for an automatic monthly deduction plan with a mutual fund company to create regular deposits into an IRA. You can even set up an automatic deduction for U.S. Savings bonds at its Web site. The whole point to this is to get the money out of your checking account as quickly as possible, before you see it and spend it.

4. Create money savings and investment goals.

Would you like to have $1 million by the age of 40 or 50 or by the time you retire? Sure you would! Begin by setting your own goals. Never set a goal you can't control. Your targets can't depend on your boss giving you a raise; they must be reachable by your own efforts. You might need to invest in yourself by acquiring more education or training so you can qualify for a job that pays more.

You might need to take more risk in your investments or in your lifestyle by taking on a second job that pays commissions instead of a fixed salary. Evaluate the risks involved, and understand that by putting the odds on your side, you can get a larger return.

CHAPTER 10- TRACK YOUR SPENDING AGAINST YOUR SET BUDGET

Budgeting and tracking your spending is all about planning your financial present and future. It's among the most essential steps that you should take for it is a fundamental aspect of your financial planning. Such planning entails establishing or setting specific goals – whether your goals are to pay off your debts or to save enough money. You basically need to fully understand your habits of spending.

The real importance of tracking your habits of spending and budgeting is about living within the limit of your paycheck and sticking with your spending goals. This can prove to be extremely rewarding, both financially and emotionally.

A good budget plan is created to last all through the years. Yes, you can actually budget for a short term basis to get your way through challenging times, but the most effective budget plans will definitely take you and your family out of big financial trouble and of course, to your financial goals. Budgeting is one of the most essential aspects of planning for your future indeed.

Creating a budget plan is at the core of your financial freedom. If you don't have such a plan to budget or track your spending, chance is things might get out of control. Once this situation happens, it's much harder for you to get things back on their track than if you'd followed a budget plan in the first place.

But how one makes a budget? Where can you begin your budgeting process?

Create a list of your income and expenses – The very first step that you should do in making a budget plan is to create a list. First, list your incomes. It's essential to include all income sources. Even the smallest interest checks should be included as well. These little things definitely add up, and to have a specific picture of the income is very critical.

Next, list all the regular bills. These may include your mortgage, home and auto insurance, water, electric, cable, phone, and other monthly bills. List when these bills are due as well as how much they cost. If it quite fluctuates, write average amounts.

After listing the regular bills, you must account for other kinds of expenses. This means expenses like gas, groceries, clothes, personal items, haircuts, among others. It's also essential that you budget your fun things such as movies, eating out, stamp collecting, or any other variables. If you do not budget your money for these things, then you'll become disillusioned eventually giving up on the budget.

Find Areas That You Can Actually Cut Back A Bit – Now that you've listed your income and expenses. Take the total expenses; subtract this from the total income. The difference will be an amount which you're under or over budget.

If you're over the budget, this means that you're spending way more than what you make. This is not ideal. For most, that overage may end up to credit cards. Then you're paying interest and this isn't actually necessary. You should always avoid using credit card in order to supplement the income.

Take the amount that's over; see where you can try to cut back from your budget. Sometimes, this could mean making a hard choice and you may need to give up something. But at the end, the reward could be worth it.

While some think that a budget plan is a constraint, but it's giving you the freedom from worry and stress from finances.

Change How You Think about Money

Most people believe that the most important step to financial freedom or to get rid of debts is to devise a budget plan or cut out the expenses. The next important step should be to invest and save. These are considered the most important steps to have successful financial goals. However, without essentially changing your mindset about money, it will be hard to attain as well as to maintain such goals.

Wondering how successful people think? How can someone develop such a mindset that can help in getting successful financial results? Well, changing your mindset about money can be the best key.

Every Cent Counts!

First, you need to completely revitalize and change your thinking. If your 'thinking' and 'actions' haven't gotten you any financial result that you always want, then it's time for you to make some changes. Deciding to change is very easy, however, to implement this change needs sincere commitment. The economic state has no actually influence to whether you will be able to be financially successful or not.

Provided this fact, it's no doubt that having a millionaire's mindset is indeed a choice and decision. You should make firm decisions for you to be the anchor for achieving your financial goals. Most successful people have strong resolve and unwavering commitments of following actions that can lead to accomplishing their financial goals.

In addition to that, you should also learn how to develop a sense of mastery in making your money grow. How can you achieve this? You must make some actions to educated yourself about turning financial resources to continuous investment cycle. Change you mindset, turn you constant having of spending into constant investing to help increase your finances.

To turn you mind to be a millionaire's mindset, begin by brainstorming different ways on how to increase the accumulation of your money. Learning is definitely one of the keys to changing your mindset. Do not be intimidated with learning things that you're unfamiliar with. This is integral parts of the processes of learning, molding, and changing your mindset about money. The more things you learn, your mind will easily conform to new ideas. Your ethic of hard work can lead you to become a master in growing your money.

If you have few limited beliefs and mindset about money, improving your finances and wealth will never become a priority for you. Precise, true, clear mindset about money will definitely establish wealth limit much higher. If you really want to achieve financial freedom for you and your family, changing your mindset towards money can be the best decision.

To open your life into abundance that is always there, you should try something new, sure, and surprising. You know that your money isn't static, it's a flow, coming, and even going out. You should improve your thinking; it will eventually free you to receive money in a spectacular way.

Be Committed to Your Plan

No one can emphasize fully how essential it really is to be committed to their plans, but way beyond this, you should commit yourself to your plans especially your financial plans. Most people spend endless time talking more about their goals and never able to do it.

Why? It is simple. They do not take the necessary steps to move forward and also, they do not commit themselves to their plans.

Commitment is one of the most important factors that contribute to successful financial goals. For you to be able to develop result oriented financial plans, you should be committed.

Serious financial goals can't be taken too lightly. Goals like financial freedom, owning your own successful business, and to live a prosperous life are serious goals and need certain committed actions in order to be accomplished. The secret to achieving your financial goals is commitment – something that is very straightforward but not easy to do.

Every Cent Counts!

Writing down all your goals is and act as well as demonstration that you are committed. You are saying to the world and to yourself that is what you really want. Well, if you really want to achieve something and if you are prepared to do what it takes to achieve those goals, there is no one and something that can easily stop you. That is what you called – commitment.

You plan on achieving something; you have identified your goals, and even working your way to that direction. Now what? Can something stop you? Certainly not! Why? It's because you are totally committed to these goals. Yes! It's your commitment that will decide the outcome.

Rest assured managing your finances requires dedication, vigilance, and commitment. After all, you are a human – from time to time things might slip out of your hand. Not just that, success also requires hard work, discipline, tenacity, perseverance, courage, will, and faith. With these in mind, you will be able to successfully achieve your goals in life.

As you develop undying commitment to achieving your goals, failures and roadblocks are merely humps and not stop signs. You goals need to be that great to feed and ignite yourself with meaning and purpose. So, if you are ready to achieve those financial goals, reestablish your commitment and see yourself succeed.

ABOUT THE AUTHOR

Sharon Turner is a financial expert who offers valuable pieces of advice to her clientele from all over the world. She works from a home office and reaches out to people of different nationalities to help them start saving.

Sharon is a single-mom to 1-year-old Josh.

www.ingramcontent.com/pod-product-compliance
Lightning Source LLC
Chambersburg PA
CBHW051244170526
45165CB00004B/1570